The Woman's Handbook
Everything You Want to Say to Your Daughter,
Sister, Niece, Friend in One Simple Book

by

Becky Due

If you purchased this book without a cover you should be aware that this book is stolen property. It was reported as "unsold and destroyed" to the publisher and neither the author nor the publisher has received any payment for this "stripped book."

This book is a work of fiction. Names, characters, places and incidents are either the product of the author's imagination or are used fictitiously. Any resemblance to actual persons, living or dead, or to actual events or locales is entirely coincidental.

THE WOMAN'S HANDBOOK: EVERYTHING YOU WANT TO SAY TO YOUR DAUGHTER, SISTER, NIECE, FRIEND IN ONE SIMPLE BOOK
COPYRIGHT © 2012 BY BECKY DUE. All rights reserved, including the right to reproduce this book, or portions thereof, in any form. No part of this text may be reproduced, transmitted, downloaded, decompiled, reverse engineered, or stored in or introduced into any information storage and retrieval system, in any form or by any means, whether electronic or mechanical without the express written permission of the author. The scanning, uploading, and distribution of this book via the Internet or via any other means without the permission of the publisher is illegal and punishable by law. Please purchase only authorized electronic editions and do not participate in or encourage electronic piracy of copyrighted materials.

The publisher does not have any control over and does not assume any responsibility for author or third-party websites or their content.

Cover Designed by Becky Due

Published by Telemachus Press, LLC
http://www.telemachuspress.com

Visit the author website
http://www.BeckyDue.com

ISBN: 978-1-937698-67-6 (eBook)
ISBN: 978-1-937698-68-3 (Paperback)

Version 2012.04.04

Printed in the United States of America

10 9 8 7 6 5 4 3 2 1

Dedicated to every woman—
Dedicated to you.

The Woman's Handbook covers the three most important parts of our lives: ourselves, our relationships, and our purpose—which should always be our passion.

You can read The Woman's Handbook from beginning to end or randomly open this book for a quick boost whenever you need inspiration.

Table of Contents

Self   1

Relationships   103

Passion, Purpose, Career   155

The Woman's Handbook
Everything You Want to Say to Your Daughter,
Sister, Niece, Friend in One Simple Book

Self ...

Enjoy your life—you only have one.

Finish school and keep learning.

Take pride in your appearance: Dress well, stand up straight, keep your shoulders back and be proud that you are a strong woman.

Don't waste your energy hating anybody.

Focus on your good qualities.

Stay true to your morals and values.

*Don't compare yourself to others
unless you are looking for inspiration.*

Get familiar with your body—know your body.

Accept rejection—it's almost always a good thing.

*Pretty or not, it is not about your looks—
it's all about what's inside.*

Do not disconnect from the reality of the hurting women who are on the streets, in prostitution, inside strip clubs, and doing pornography.

Pay your bills on time.

Don't be prejudiced.

*Get rid of the clutter around you
that weighs you down.*

Take good care of your skin.

Allow yourself bad days.

Don't generalize about people.

Take a powernap when you can.

Feel your feelings—allow yourself to be angry or sad but don't stay there too long.

You can always change your life simply by changing your mind.

Don't sleep with married men.

*Be brave, take risks, stay courageous,
and go for your big dreams.*

If you drink, make sure you are safe.

Be on time.

Sometimes making a decision is the best decision so you can move on with your life.

*Don't strike another person unless it's in
self-defense; then do what it takes
to protect yourself and survive.*

Stay aware of body language.

Live what you want your legacy to be.

Be grateful for all the good in your life today.

If you were victimized as a child, it was not your fault. You didn't do anything to deserve it. If you're still struggling, tell somebody you trust and get help.

Take a self-defense class.

Don't turn your feelings inward against yourself or you could end up with depression.

*Fill your own cup first,
and then give freely what you have left to give.*

Sometimes you can only take it one minute, one hour, one day at a time.

Don't drink, overeat, take drugs, or create an addiction to avoid or numb emotional pain— talk, journal, get help.

Give yourself what you most want from others.

Take care of yourself and have good hygiene.

Focus on your needs more than your wants.

Don't bully or be a part of bullying; instead, stand up for those who need your help.

Hold out for sex.

Know where you stand with politics and religion.

Forgive others.

Make time to be outside with nature.

Respect authority.

Always have goals.

You are a woman first, and then you are a wife, mother, daughter, sister, or friend.

Take full responsibility for your life.

Learn to laugh at yourself.

Stay confident.

You are stronger than what happens to you.

*Keep your personal space organized,
clean, and safe.*

There is always somebody worse off than you are, so if you're feeling down about your life, reach out and help somebody else.

Don't make a habit of procrastination.

Keep your credit score high.

Live a happy life—smile, have fun, and laugh.

Stick up for yourself.

When you make a mistake, don't beat yourself up—mistakes build character.

See a doctor when you have a concern.

Don't let fear run your life.

Support other women.

Vote.

Expect and accept change.

*Stand for something,
so you don't fall for everything.*

*Don't break the law, but if you do, admit it,
accept the consequences,
and learn from the experience.*

*Visualize your dream life—
visualize what you want.*

Don't do drugs.

Do monthly breast self-exams.

*Small steps in the right direction
will improve your life.*

Ask for help when you need it. Reaching out for help is a true sign of strength.

Enjoy your own company when you're alone.

*Don't let hurt or anger turn inward
and make you bitter or sick;
instead, use it as fuel
to drive you to something better.*

If you run into a problem, get the facts, don't worry, be strong, and know that you're going to get through this.

Keep your self-dialogue positive.

Stay aware of your surroundings—stay safe.

There is nobody in the world like you.

If you're going to drink, drink responsibly.

Remember that the greatest revenge is a life well-lived.

Cry when you need to.

Don't smoke.

Speak up—your voice is important.

Life is all about choices—be responsible for your choices and make choices based on what you want your life to be.

Take control of your life—you have the power to make your dreams come true.

Don't wait to be rescued—rescue yourself.

Follow rules and laws.

Make your own money.

Take moments to sit in silence.

Don't drink and drive.

Skinny or not, it is not about your body—it's all about how you feel.

Protect yourself.

If your past is holding you back, get help.

Make decisions based on your values.

Some things are just not meant to be.

Trust yourself to handle everything that comes your way—be gentle with yourself, have faith, and trust that everything happens for a reason.

Don't blame others when you make a mistake.

Remember that happiness is a choice.

*Stay healthy, fit, and active—get enough sleep,
make healthy food choices,
drink plenty of water, and exercise.*

Trust your intuition.

Don't act like or pretend you are less than you are.

Forgive yourself.

You are amazing.

Relationships ...

Make a list of non-negotiable traits in a partner. For example, he must:

- *be faithful and loyal*
- *have a sense of humor*
- *accept my family and friends*
- *be tolerant of my quirks and moods*
- *respect women*
- *live a healthy lifestyle*
- *be financially secure (a.k.a. have a job)*
- *be independent and give me space*
- *have faith in a higher power*

Make sure you have the same traits you expect from your future partner.

*Don't depend on somebody else
to make you happy.*

A win for your friend is always a win for you.

Imagine failed relationships as steppingstones to something better.

Women and men are more alike than different—we want the same things.

- *We want to feel important.*
- *We want to be appreciated.*
- *We want to know we are valuable.*
- *We want to love.*
- *We want to be loved.*

Be there for people you love.

Stick with people who challenge you to do and be better.

If you do something wrong, admit it.

*Don't waste your time, money, and energy
helping people who have no interest
in improving their lives.*

Be trustworthy—tell the truth, keep promises, and keep your friends' secrets.

*If a man hits you, walk. The longer you stay,
the harder it is to leave ...
and the abuse always gets worse.*

Nobody makes it on their own.

Always trust a person's actions more than you trust their words.

You are never alone when you have family and friends.

If in an argument, stay focused on the real issues and own your part of the problem.

*Meet new people and be open
to new relationships.*

Take your power back from anybody who has mistreated you by becoming better, stronger, happier than them.

All the little girls around you are watching and learning from you.

*Don't change who you are
to please somebody else.*

*Protect your heart,
but still take chances with love.*

It's better to want somebody than to need them.

Hang out with likeminded women.

Always use protection.

Set boundaries and keep boundaries.

Listen to your parents—they may be wrong but still always listen.

*Don't give yourself, your life,
or your power to somebody else.*

Face your fear.

Your family may be your best friends.

The right mate will never make you cry.

*Discover something important about yourself
from every relationship.*

If you stay a victim, you have given up and you have given your power to your victimizer—you are way too strong to be a victim in your life.

*Always trust yourself more
than you trust others.*

Don't try to change people.

When you're feeling overwhelmed by the people around you, disengage and get some space.

If you hurt somebody, apologize.

Avoid becoming a doormat by keeping your morals and values intact.

Don't start a new relationship until your past pains have healed.

Even when your weeks get busy, still find time to spend with your best friends.

Surround yourself with strong, successful, happy women.

Don't stay in abusive, unhealthy, unhappy, one-sided, loveless relationships.

Be happy if you have one or two close friends.

*Healthy relationships are sometimes hard work,
but it beats the alternative of isolation.*

Ask your family and friends for help when you're struggling.

Don't let a man—or anyone—pressure you into doing something you are not comfortable with.

Have compassion, put yourself in their shoes, and try to understand.

Detach from people who are bringing you down.

No partner is perfect; perfection is in the unity.

*Don't want somebody
who doesn't want you back.*

*You're going to need your friends,
so keep them in your life.*

Passion, Purpose, Career ...

Find a job you love so it doesn't feel like work.

*Be gracious, supportive, and, most of all,
motivated when a friend, co-worker,
or colleague moves ahead.*

Take a deep breath and say, "I trust myself and I know that I can manage every difficulty in front of me."

Pay your own bills.

*Achievements—big and small—
transform your life.*

Don't be afraid to fail.

Prioritize what is important, and do first what will get you to your goal.

Own your actions and take responsibility for your work.

Believe in yourself.

*Follow your talents
to where your talents lead you.*

Get inspiration from the women who came before you.

*Work hard, but take breaks
to enjoy the rewards.*

If you're not happy with your job, find a new job that will get you closer to your future career.

Avoid co-workers who make you feel less than you are.

Have a strong work ethic.

*When you experience failure or rejection, it just means that there is
now opportunity for another door to open.*

Don't sell yourself short.

Use frustration as a tool to motivate you to climb the ladder of success.

*Appreciate your career
but continue to strive for more.*

Encourage other women to dream big.

You can be whatever you want, but it will take hard work and dedication.

*Don't dwell on mistakes—
learn from them and move on.*

Be confident in your decisions.

*Never let somebody hold you back
from what you want.*

*When you're overwhelmed
or over-worked, delegate.*

Don't be afraid to succeed.

Don't procrastinate—focus on how you'll feel once the task is complete.

Tomorrow is a new day and a new challenge.

If you think you're falling behind, go back to school or take a class—educate yourself.

*Stay loyal to yourself
as you succeed in your career.*

Enjoy the people you work with.

Take one step at a time.

Continue to set new career goals.

Stay focused.

Stick with goal-oriented women.

Divide your big goals into small, reachable mini-goals.

*Force yourself to do better;
challenge yourself.*

Strong, brave, courageous women are not afraid of rejection or failure.

*Don't burn bridges when you leave one office,
job, or career to move forward.*

Do first what will get you to your goal.

There is always a team of people behind one person's success.

*If you know your purpose,
everything else falls into place.*

Don't let setbacks discourage you, because every successful person has them.

Take a break when you need to recharge your batteries.

Your career may change as you change.

*Make a list of your goals
and stay focused on achieving them.*

Don't give up.

Stay ethical.

You will have bad days, but you're strong enough to get through it.

Find your purpose for being on this earth and make that your career.

If you enjoyed
The Woman's Handbook
*Everything You Want to Say to Your Daughter,
Sister, Niece, Friend in One Simple Book*
why not try other great titles by
Becky Due?

You can find Becky Due at:

www.BeckyDue.com
www.facebook.com/BeckyDue.Author
www.twitter.com/BeckyDue
http://BeckyDue.wordpress.com

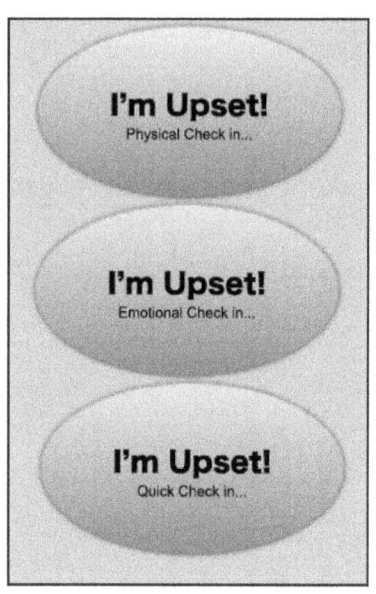

I'm Upset! App

Available at
iTunes App Store for only $0.99

I'm Upset! is like having your two best friends in your purse, with you at all times—one who gives you Tough Love and one who is more about the Gentle Love.

It doesn't matter what you're going through, *I'm Upset!* is a quick and easy way to get that needed boost when you're just not feeling right.

Don't let little upsets distract you from your awesome life. Check in with *I'm Upset!*

www.ingramcontent.com/pod-product-compliance
Lightning Source LLC
LaVergne TN
LVHW051048080426
835508LV00019B/1777